The Wealth Rewire

Reprogram Your Brain for Passive Income

Praveenraj

The Wealth Rewire: Reprogram Your Brain for Passive Income

First Edition

Published via Notion Press

Disclaimer: All character names, individuals, and scenarios described in this book are entirely fictitious. They are composites created for illustrative purposes only and do not represent any specific real person, living or dead. Any resemblance to actual individuals is purely coincidental.

Preface

This book took two years to write. Not because the writing was slow, but because the research underneath it was deep. Two years studying how psychology shapes financial behaviour. Two years reading case studies of ordinary people – not billionaires, not tech founders – who quietly built wealth that gave them freedom. What survived after cutting away the hype, the survivorship bias, and the Instagram nonsense is what you are holding now.

The material comes from behavioural finance studies, documented interviews with self-made wealth builders, and the messy reality of how people actually make decisions about money. Not textbook theory. Real patterns from real lives.

Here is what the research kept pointing to: most people are not stuck because they lack brains, opportunity, or willpower. They are stuck because their thinking is wired wrong. Wired for consumption, not creation. For earning, not building. For spending every raise instead of compounding it. These patterns get installed in childhood and run silently in the background for decades – unless you catch them and rewire them deliberately.

That is what this book does. Chapter by chapter, it pulls apart the mental habits that keep people trapped in the earn-spend cycle, and replaces them with the frameworks that quietly wealthy people actually live by. No rah-rah motivation. Just clear, practical shifts in how you see income, time, and value — backed by evidence, written in plain language.

The aim is to shift your default question from "How do I earn more at my job?" to "How do I build something that earns without me?" That shift is quiet. Internal. Nobody around you will notice it happening. But it changes everything that comes after.

Table of Contents

Part V: The Long Game

Closing

PART I: THE FOUNDATION

* * *

Chapter 1: The Invisible Gap

I once sat next to a retired naval officer at a dinner party. His name was George. He was seventy-three, wore a cardigan that had seen better days, and drove a twelve-year-old Volvo. Somewhere in the conversation, between the roast potatoes and dessert, he mentioned – almost as an afterthought – that he owned fourteen washing machines.

Not a laundrette. Just fourteen commercial washing machines, placed in student accommodation buildings around Portsmouth. Each one earned a few pounds a day. Nothing glamorous. Nothing that would make anyone's eyes widen at a cocktail party. But together, quietly, month after month, those machines produced enough income to cover his mortgage, his groceries, and his modest lifestyle. George hadn't worked in eight years. He slept well. He travelled when he felt like it. He was, by any honest measure, wealthy.

At that same dinner sat a woman named Caroline. She was a litigation partner at a well-known London firm. She earned a figure that most people would consider extraordinary. She wore beautiful clothes. She drove a German car that cost more than George's entire washing machine operation. And she confided to me, after her third glass of wine, that she hadn't taken a proper holiday in two years because she couldn't afford to — not in terms of time, but in terms of money. Her mortgage, her children's school fees, her car payments, and the general cost of maintaining the life that someone at her level was supposed to live had consumed everything. Every month was tight. She was one bad quarter away from genuine financial stress.

Here were two people at the same table. One earned a fraction of the other. But only one of them was free.

That evening changed how I thought about money. Not because I suddenly understood investing or business or compound interest. But because I finally saw the gap. The invisible gap.

Wealth is not what you earn. It is the distance between what your money produces without you and what your life costs to maintain. That's it. That's the whole thing. Everything else is detail.

George had a small income that required almost none of his time, and a life that cost very little. Caroline had a large income that required all of her time, and a life that cost nearly every penny of it. On paper, Caroline was richer. In reality, George was wealthier. And that distinction matters more than almost anything else in this book.

I want you to meet someone. His name is Alex. He's not a real person — he's a composite, built from dozens of people I've known, worked with, and learned from over the years. Alex is thirty-one. He works in operations for a mid-sized company. He earns a decent salary. Not spectacular, not terrible. Enough to pay rent, run a car, and put a little aside most months.

Alex is good at his job. His manager likes him. He gets solid performance reviews. But lately, something has been nagging at him. A quiet thought that surfaces on Sunday evenings and during his commute. It goes something like this: is this really it? Trade forty years of Mondays for a pension and a watch? Hope that the company doesn't restructure, that his knees hold out, that the cost of living doesn't outpace his pay rises?

Alex isn't ungrateful. He knows plenty of people who would love his job. But he has this growing suspicion that there might be another way. Not a reckless, quit-your-job-and-follow-your-passion way. Something more measured. Something that a careful, slightly anxious person could actually do.

This book is for Alex. And if you're reading this, it's probably for you too.

There are really two paths to building wealth. The first is the traditional path: earn a salary, spend less than you earn, invest the difference, wait thirty years, and let compound interest do its thing. This path works. It's boring, it's slow, and it absolutely works. I will never tell you to ignore it.

The second path is the accelerated path: build something that earns money alongside your job. Create income that doesn't require your presence. Develop skills that the market pays handsomely for. Use that extra income to save and invest more aggressively, which makes the traditional path work faster.

This book is about both paths. Because the truth is, you don't choose one or the other. The smartest people I know walk both paths at the same time. They invest every month, rain or shine. And they also build. They tinker. They experiment. They quietly assemble something on the side that, over time, changes the shape of their financial life.

The key word there is quietly. This isn't a book about becoming a celebrity entrepreneur or building the next tech unicorn. This is a book about the wealth rewire — the kind of wealth-building that happens in the margins. Early mornings. Lunch breaks. Evenings after the kids are asleep. Saturdays when everyone else is watching football.

It's not loud. It's not flashy. But it works. And the people who do it well tend to sleep as soundly as George.

Let's begin.

* * *

Chapter 2: The Stories We Inherit

Before we talk about money, we need to talk about the stories you already believe about money. Because you do believe stories about it. We all do. And most of them were installed before you were old enough to question them.

I grew up hearing certain phrases so often that they became invisible. "Money doesn't grow on trees." "We're not made of money." "People like us don't do things like that." My parents weren't trying to damage me. They were passing on what they knew, which was passed to them by their parents, who had their own fears and their own scarcity. It's an inheritance, just not the kind anyone puts in a will.

Here's what I've noticed after years of paying attention to this: the stories you inherit about money shape your financial life more powerfully than your salary, your education, or your intelligence. I've met brilliant people who are broke because deep down they believe that wanting money makes you greedy. I've met people with modest educations who are genuinely wealthy because they grew up around the assumption that building something of your own was simply what you did.

The script you were handed matters. And the first step in building wealth is figuring out what your script says.

Some people were told that money is scarce and dangerous. That having too much of it changes you for the worse. That wealthy people got that way by taking advantage of others. If that's your inherited story, then every time you start to earn more, a part of your brain will quietly sabotage things. It will feel safer to stay where you are. To not want too much. To keep your head down.

Other people were told that talking about money is vulgar. That ambition is something to be embarrassed about. That the proper thing to do is get a respectable job, live within your means, and never, ever appear to be trying too hard. This one runs deep in certain cultures. It ran deep in mine.

I had a friend – I'll call him Darren – who was offered a freelance project that would have paid him more in six weeks than he earned in three months at his day job. A company wanted him to redesign their onboarding process. He had exactly the right skills. The timeline was generous. The money was genuinely life-changing for where he was at the time.

He turned it down.

When I asked him why, he said something I've never forgotten. "I don't want people to think I'm one of those hustler types." He said it casually, like it was obvious. Like the risk of someone raising an eyebrow at him was more dangerous than passing up the money.

I didn't argue with him at the time. But I've thought about that moment a lot since. Because Darren's fear wasn't about the work. It wasn't about the client. It was about being seen. About stepping out of the identity that felt safe and familiar. About doing something that the people around him might not understand or approve of.

This is the number one barrier I see. Not lack of money. Not lack of ideas. Not lack of time. The fear of being seen doing something different. Most people will sacrifice their financial future to avoid a raised eyebrow from someone whose opinion, if they're honest, doesn't actually matter that much.

I want to say something about that, and I want to say it plainly: the people who will judge you for building something are almost always people who aren't building anything themselves. Their discomfort is not your responsibility. And their approval is not worth what it costs you.

There's another inherited story I hear constantly. It goes like this: "The market is saturated. Everyone is already doing that. There's too much competition. It's too late."

I once met a woman named Helen who ran a small bookkeeping practice in Leeds. She served about thirty clients, mostly local shops and tradespeople. When I suggested she could grow by offering a slightly more specialised service to a specific type of business – say, restaurants – she shook her head. "There are already loads of bookkeepers doing that," she said.

I asked her how many of her current clients had found her through a Google search. She said none. They'd all come through word of mouth, one at a time, over several years. I asked her how many restaurant owners in Leeds she thought were currently looking for a bookkeeper who actually understood their industry — someone who knew about stock wastage, seasonal cash flow, and staff tip reporting. She paused. "Probably quite a few, actually."

Helen's story is common. The presence of competitors doesn't mean the opportunity is gone. It means the demand is proven. It means people are already paying for this thing. That's good news, not bad news. The bookkeeper who specialises in restaurants isn't competing with every other bookkeeper. She's the obvious choice for a very specific group of people. And that specificity is worth far more than trying to be everything to everyone.

You will carry your inherited stories forward until you choose to examine them. I can't do that work for you. But I can tell you this: every wealthy person I've ever met had to, at some point, disagree with a story they were told as a child. Every single one.

Here's a simple exercise that might help. Take a piece of paper and write down every phrase about money that you heard regularly growing up. Don't censor yourself. Just let them come. "Money is the root of all evil." "Rich people are selfish." "You have to work hard for every penny." "Don't get above your station." Write them all down.

Now look at that list. Those are the rules you've been playing by, whether you realised it or not. Some of them might be useful. Some of them are almost certainly holding you back. You get to decide which ones to keep and which ones to leave behind. That choice — the conscious decision to write your own script — is where financial independence actually begins. Not with a spreadsheet. Not with an investment account. With a decision about what you believe.

It's uncomfortable. It's meant to be. Do it anyway.

* * *

Chapter 3: The Traps That Keep People Broke

I debated whether to put this chapter so early in the book. Part of me wanted to get straight to the exciting stuff – the skills, the strategies, the stories of people who built something remarkable. But then I thought about all the people I've watched stumble over the same avoidable mistakes, year after year, and I decided that honesty upfront is worth more than enthusiasm.

This chapter is about traps. Not the dramatic, headline-grabbing kind. The quiet kind. The ones that feel like progress while they slowly steal your time. I've fallen into most of them myself, so there's no judgement here. Just recognition, and hopefully, a way through.

The "Perfect Plan" Trap

I spent seven months once working on a business plan. Seven months. I had spreadsheets. I had market analysis. I had a logo designed. I had a colour palette chosen. I had a name, a tagline, and a twelve-page document that described, in precise detail, what my business would look like once it launched.

It never launched.

The plan was so detailed, so polished, so complete that by the time I finished it, I was exhausted. I'd spent all my creative energy on the preparation and had nothing left for the doing. Worse, the plan had become a kind of shield. As long as I was "still planning," I didn't have to face the terrifying possibility that the market might not care about my idea.

Here's what I've learned since: no plan survives contact with the market. The business you imagine at your kitchen table is never the business that actually works. The real business reveals itself only after you start talking to actual people, making actual offers, and receiving actual feedback. Planning feels productive. But past a certain point – and that point arrives much sooner than you think – it becomes a sophisticated form of avoidance.

You need a plan. But you need a simple one. Who are you helping? What problem are you solving? How will people find you? How will they pay you? That's enough to start. Everything else you'll figure out as you go. And you'll figure it out faster by doing than by planning.

The Shiny Object Trap

Three weeks. That's roughly how long the average person sticks with a new idea before something shinier comes along.

I know this because I used to be that person. One month I was going to start a copywriting business. The next month I'd seen someone on the internet making money with print-on-demand t-shirts, so I pivoted to that. Two weeks later, someone told me about Amazon FBA and suddenly I was researching wholesale suppliers. Then someone mentioned property investing and I spent a weekend calculating mortgage yields. None of these things are bad ideas. But I never gave any of them enough time to actually work.

Social media makes this worse. Every day, your feed shows you someone who's succeeded at something you haven't tried yet. And your brain does this subtle, poisonous thing — it makes you feel like you're falling behind. Like the thing you're working on is too slow, too boring, too ordinary. Like that other person found the shortcut and you're stuck on the long road.

The truth is almost always the opposite. The person who succeeded stuck with one thing long enough for it to compound. They had the same doubts you have. They saw the same shiny objects. They just didn't chase them.

My rule now — and it's one I'd encourage you to steal — is one hundred days. If you start something, you commit to it for one hundred days before you're allowed to evaluate whether it's working. Not three weeks. Not six weeks. One hundred days. That's enough time for the initial excitement to fade, for the hard middle to reveal itself, and for the first real signals of success or failure to emerge.

Most things that work don't feel like they're working at the sixty-day mark. That's normal. Keep going.

The "I Need More Information" Trap

I have a friend who has been "learning about investing" for four years. He's read eleven books. He's taken three online courses. He listens to two podcasts about it every week. He can explain the difference between index funds and actively managed funds with genuine expertise.

He has invested exactly zero pounds.

This is the information trap, and it's one of the most comfortable prisons you can build for yourself. Because learning feels like progress. Each book, each course, each video gives you that small rush of understanding. You feel like you're getting closer. But closer to what? If you never act on what you've learned, you haven't educated yourself. You've entertained yourself.

Information without action is entertainment, not education. Education changes your behaviour. Entertainment fills your time.

I'm not against learning. Obviously. I wrote a book, for heaven's sake. But I am against using learning as a substitute for doing. And the way to tell the difference is simple: if you've consumed more than three pieces of content on a topic without taking a single real-world action, you're hiding. You have enough information. What you lack is not knowledge. It's nerve.

The next piece of content you consume should be your own — a first attempt, a first conversation with a potential client, a first terrible draft. That's where the real learning lives.

The Overnight Success Myth

Social media has a compression problem. You scroll through your feed and you see someone celebrating their first six-figure year. What you don't see is the two years before that — the months of zero revenue, the failed launches, the ideas that went nowhere, the evenings spent working after the kids went to bed while nothing seemed to be happening.

The internet shows you outcomes. It almost never shows you timelines.

Here is what a realistic timeline actually looks like for most people who build something meaningful alongside their day job. In the first one to three months, you're figuring things out. You're choosing what to offer. You're talking to people. You're making mistakes. Revenue is likely zero, or close to it.

From months three to six, you start getting traction. Maybe your first paying client. Maybe a few small wins. The money is inconsistent and modest. Some months are encouraging. Some months make you wonder why you're bothering.

From months six to twelve, things start to make more sense. You understand what works and what doesn't. You've refined your offer. Your income from this side work is real but probably not life-changing yet. Maybe a few hundred pounds in a quiet month, maybe a couple of thousand in a good one.

From years one to two, you're building momentum. If you've stuck with it – and most people haven't, which is exactly why the ones who do get rewarded – the income becomes more consistent. It starts to feel like a real thing rather than an experiment.

From years two to three, you could realistically be earning enough to replace your salary, if that's your goal. Some people reach this point sooner. Some take longer. Both are fine.

From year five onward, if you've been consistent, you're likely in a position that would have seemed impossible when you started. Not because you did anything extraordinary. But because you didn't stop.

That's the real timeline. It's not glamorous. It won't get a million views on social media. But it's honest, and it's achievable, and it's the path that almost every quietly wealthy person I know has actually walked.

The "I'll Start When..." Trap

I'll start when I have more savings. I'll start when the kids are older. I'll start when I finish this course. I'll start when the economy improves. I'll start when I feel ready.

I've heard every version of this. I've said most of them myself. And they all have one thing in common: they sound responsible while being the opposite. They feel like wisdom. But they're fear wearing a sensible outfit.

There is never a perfect time to start. The economy is always uncertain. The kids will always need something. You will never feel ready, because readiness is not a feeling – it's a decision.

I started my first real side project during one of the busiest periods of my life. I had a demanding job, a new flat that needed work, and about a dozen reasons why "now" was the wrong time. But I'd run out of patience with my own excuses. So I started badly, with imperfect conditions, in stolen hours. And it worked. Not because the timing was right. But because I finally stopped waiting for it to be.

If you're reading this book, you have enough. Enough time, enough knowledge, enough resources to take the first step. Not the tenth step. The first one. Start messy. Start small. Start scared. Just start.

The Comparison Trap

There is a particular kind of misery that comes from comparing your beginning to someone else's middle. And social media serves it to you on a silver platter, every single day.

You see someone three years into their journey, posting about their wins, and you feel like a failure because you haven't even started. Or you're three months in, earning almost nothing, and you see someone at your level who seems to be flying. You don't know their full story. You don't know what advantages they started with, what sacrifices they're making, or what struggles they're not posting about.

Comparison is a thief. It steals your motivation and replaces it with shame. And the cruelest part is that it's usually based on incomplete information. You're comparing your behind-the-scenes footage with someone else's highlight reel.

The only comparison that matters is this: are you further along than you were three months ago? If yes, you're doing fine. If no, something needs to change. That's it. Everyone else's journey is irrelevant to yours.

The "Get Rich Quick" Trap

Every few years, a new version of this appears. Sometimes it's a cryptocurrency that's going to make early investors millionaires. Sometimes it's a multi-level marketing scheme disguised as an "opportunity." Sometimes it's a course that promises passive income with no effort, no skills, and no risk.

The pattern is always the same. Big promises. Urgent language. A suggestion that you need to act now before the window closes. Testimonials from people who got in early. And a price tag that's just high enough to feel like a serious investment but just low enough to seem accessible.

I won't spend long on this because the principle is simple. If something promises exceptional returns with minimal effort and minimal risk, it is almost certainly a trap. Real wealth is boring. It's built slowly, through skills, service, saving, and patience. It doesn't make for exciting social media content. But it's real, and it lasts.

The people selling get-rich-quick schemes are getting rich by selling get-rich-quick schemes. That's usually the only business model that's actually working.

The Lifestyle Inflation Trap

This is the quietest trap of all, and possibly the most dangerous. Because it doesn't feel like a trap. It feels like reward.

You get a raise. You deserve it — you've been working hard. So you upgrade your car. You move to a slightly nicer flat. You start eating out more. You buy better clothes. Each upgrade is small and reasonable on its own. But collectively, they consume the entire raise. Your income went up, but your gap didn't. You're earning more and you're still in exactly the same position.

I watched this happen to a colleague over the course of about five years. Every promotion, every pay rise, every bonus — consumed. Not by extravagance. By small, incremental lifestyle upgrades that each felt perfectly justified. At the end of those five years, he was earning nearly twice what he'd started at. His savings rate was actually lower. He was running faster and falling further behind.

The antidote is simple but not easy. When your income goes up, your lifestyle should stay roughly the same — at least for a while. The gap between what you earn and what you spend is the single most important number in your financial life. Protect it. Grow it. That gap is your freedom, measured in pounds and pence.

So What Does A Realistic First Year Actually Look Like?

I want to end this chapter with honesty, because I think you deserve it.

If you start building something alongside your day job — a freelance skill, a small service, a side business — your first year will probably look something like this.

The first few months will be messy. You'll second-guess yourself constantly. You'll wonder if you've chosen the right thing. You'll compare yourself to people who seem further along. Your income from this new thing will be zero or negligible.

Around the middle of the year, things will start to click. Not dramatically. Not in a way that makes for a good story. But you'll get your first client, or your first sale, or your first piece of genuine positive feedback. And something inside you will shift. You'll realise this might actually work.

By the end of the first year, if you've been consistent — and that's a big if, because most people aren't — you might be earning anywhere from a few hundred to a couple of thousand pounds a month from your side work. Some months will be great. Some months will be nothing. The average will be modest.

And that's fine. That's good. That's progress. Because in year two, with everything you've learned, you'll move faster. And in year three, faster still.

The people who build real wealth aren't the ones who had the best first year. They're the ones who didn't quit after a mediocre one.

* * *

Chapter 4: The Courage to Start

Alex sat in the same office chair for four years.

Not the same physical chair – the company moved offices twice during that time. But the same metaphorical chair. The same role, the same routine, the same vague feeling on Sunday evenings that something was missing. He'd think about starting something. He'd research ideas online. He'd bookmark articles with titles like "50 Side Hustles You Can Start This Weekend." And then Monday would arrive, the week would swallow him whole, and the idea would drift back to wherever half-formed ambitions go to wait.

Four years. That's roughly two hundred Sundays of the same quiet restlessness. The same cycle of inspiration and inaction.

I tell you this not to make Alex sound weak. He wasn't. He was careful, which is different. Careful people don't leap without looking. They analyse. They weigh up. They consider what could go wrong. These are admirable traits in most areas of life. But when it comes to starting something new, they can become a prison. Because there will always be another risk to consider, another variable to account for, another reason to wait just a little longer.

What finally moved Alex wasn't a dramatic moment. It wasn't a redundancy scare or a flash of inspiration or a motivational speech. It was boredom. Pure, grinding, existential boredom. The realisation that if nothing changed, nothing would change. That the safety he'd been protecting was actually a very comfortable cage.

I've found that most people don't start because of inspiration. They start because the pain of staying still finally exceeds the fear of moving. It's not elegant, but it's true.

If you're reading this and recognising yourself — the ideas that come and go, the bookmarked articles, the plans that never quite become actions — I have something for you. It's not a masterplan. It's a habit.

For the next thirty days, every time an idea enters your mind — any idea, however small or silly — do one thing about it within twenty-four hours. Not ten things. One thing. If you think "I could offer social media help to local businesses," then within twenty-four hours, send one message to one local business. If you think "I'd be good at tutoring," then within twenty-four hours, write a brief description of what you'd offer and send it to one person.

The action doesn't need to be big. It needs to be real. It needs to exist in the world, not just in your head.

Most of these actions will lead nowhere. That's the point. You're not trying to find the perfect idea on day one. You're trying to break the habit of inaction. You're training yourself to respond to ideas with movement instead of contemplation.

After thirty days of this, something interesting usually happens. One or two of those small actions will have produced a response. A conversation. A flicker of interest. Maybe even an opportunity. And you'll start to see which ideas have legs and which don't – not because you analysed them in your head, but because you tested them in the real world.

There's another test I use, and I find it remarkably reliable. I call it the fourteen-day test. When an idea first arrives, it's exciting. Everything is exciting when it's new. But most ideas fade within a week. The initial enthusiasm burns off and you're left with nothing.

The ideas that keep coming back – the ones that nag at you in the shower, that pop into your head while you're driving, that you find yourself researching even when you told yourself you'd stop – those are worth paying attention to. If an idea keeps returning after fourteen days, it's trying to tell you something. It might not be the final form of what you'll build, but it's pointing in a direction worth exploring.

Now, I want to address something that well-meaning but reckless advice often gets wrong. You've probably seen the social media posts. "Quit your job. Burn the boats. Go all in." It makes for a great story. It makes for terrible financial advice.

Here's what I believe, and what I've seen work repeatedly for people who have responsibilities and mortgages and families: build the bridge before you burn the boat.

Keep your job. Build your side income in the margins. When that side income reaches roughly sixty percent of your salary – and when it's been at that level for at least three to six months, proving it's not a fluke – then you can start thinking about making changes. Maybe you go part-time. Maybe you negotiate a different arrangement with your employer. Maybe, eventually, you leave altogether.

But you do it from a position of strength, not desperation. You do it with a bridge already built, not a prayer and a parachute.

Alex kept his job for eighteen months after he started building something on the side. During those eighteen months, he often felt impatient. He wanted to go faster. He wanted to quit and commit fully. But he didn't, because the financial security of his salary gave him something invaluable: the freedom to experiment without panic. He could try things, fail at things, and adjust his approach without the pressure of needing it to work right now.

That patience wasn't weakness. It was strategy. And when he finally did make the transition, it felt less like a leap of faith and more like stepping onto solid ground he'd been building for over a year.

There's one more thing I want to say about starting, and it's something I wish someone had told me earlier. The first version of anything you build will be embarrassing. Your first website will look amateur. Your first sales message will feel clumsy. Your first client conversation will be awkward. You'll stumble over your pricing. You'll undersell yourself. You'll make promises you're not sure you can keep.

That's normal. That's everyone. The polished, confident people you admire online were once exactly where you are. They just started earlier. And they didn't let the embarrassment of the first version stop them from getting to the fifth version, and then the twentieth.

Alex's first attempt at offering a service was, by his own admission, terrible. He wrote a LinkedIn post about what he was offering, and it was too long, too vague, and too apologetic. The response was almost nothing. Two likes and a polite comment from his mum. He wanted to delete it and pretend it never happened.

Instead, he wrote a better one the following week. And a slightly better one after that. By the sixth attempt, someone replied asking for more details. By the eighth, he had his first paying client. The first version was embarrassing. The eighth version worked. But the eighth version could never have existed without the first.

Courage doesn't always look like jumping. Sometimes it looks like building, quietly, consistently, until the jump is just a small step.

* * *

PART II: BUILDING YOUR VALUE

* * *

Chapter 5: Your Market Rate

Here's something that took me an embarrassingly long time to understand: if you have a job, you are already running a business. It's a business with one employee – you – and one client – your employer. Your salary is the price that client pays for your services. Your annual review is a client feedback meeting. Your CV is a sales brochure.

Once you see it this way, certain things become clearer. For example: why do some people with similar skills earn wildly different amounts? It's not always about who works harder or who's smarter. It's often about proximity to revenue.

Think of it like this. Inside any company, some roles are directly connected to how the company makes money. Sales, for example. Product development. Marketing that drives measurable growth. Other roles are essential but further from the revenue – administration, compliance, internal support. The roles closest to revenue almost always pay more. Not because they're harder. Not because the people in them are more valuable as humans. But because the connection between their work and the company's income is visible and direct.

This principle doesn't just apply to employment. It's the single most important thing to understand when you're deciding what to offer the market. The closer your skill is to helping someone make or save money, the more they'll pay for it.

Which brings me to a crucial distinction: selling to businesses versus selling to individuals.

When you sell to an individual – a person spending their own money – they feel every pound. They compare your price to what that money could buy them elsewhere. A fifty-pound purchase gets weighed against a nice dinner out, a new pair of shoes, a month of streaming subscriptions. The decision is emotional and deeply personal.

When you sell to a business, the calculation is completely different. A business doesn't think "that's expensive." A business thinks "will this make me more money than it costs?" If you charge a business two thousand pounds for something that helps them earn ten thousand, you're not an expense. You're an investment with a five-to-one return. They'll pay gladly and ask if you can do more.

This is why I encourage almost everyone who's starting to build something on the side to sell to businesses rather than individuals. The money is better. The conversations are more rational. And the value you create is easier to demonstrate.

Let me tell you about Priya.

Priya was twenty-three and working a standard office job in Birmingham when she noticed something. Her aunt was a dentist. She ran a busy practice, and every day she dealt with the same headaches: missed appointments, phone calls that went unanswered because the receptionist was busy, new patient enquiries that fell through the cracks, and a booking system that seemed designed to frustrate everyone who used it.

Priya didn't know anything about dentistry. But she was reasonably comfortable with technology, and she'd been reading about chatbots and automated scheduling tools. She spent about six weeks – evenings and weekends – learning how these tools worked. Not getting a degree. Not taking a twelve-month course. Just focused, practical learning. How to set up a chatbot that could answer common patient questions. How to integrate an online booking system. How to automate appointment reminders so fewer people no-showed.

She set up her aunt's practice as a test case. Within a month, her missed appointments dropped noticeably. New patient enquiries were being captured automatically instead of lost. Her receptionist was spending less time on the phone and more time on things that actually needed a human touch.

Her aunt mentioned it to a friend who ran another dental practice. That friend asked Priya if she could do the same thing for her. She could, and she did. She told two more dentists. Within six months, Priya was serving eleven dental practices, each paying her a monthly fee to maintain and improve their systems.

She was earning more than most of the dentists she served. She was twenty-three. She didn't have a business degree. She didn't have a fancy website. She didn't have investors or a startup or any of the things you might think you need.

What she had was a specific skill, applied to a specific industry, solving a specific problem. And she sold it to businesses, not individuals. That's the formula. It's not more complicated than that.

Your market rate — the amount the world is willing to pay you — is not fixed by your age, your education, or your job title. It's determined by the value you create, the specificity of your skill, and the type of buyer you serve. Change any one of those three variables and your earning potential shifts dramatically.

Most people never change any of them. They accept the rate their employer sets and assume that's what they're worth. It isn't. It's just what one buyer is currently paying. The market is much larger than your current job, and it values different things than your boss might.

There's one more thing worth understanding about your market rate. It's not just about what you charge — it's about how you frame what you do. Priya didn't describe herself as "a person who sets up chatbots." She described herself as "the person who helps dental practices never miss another new patient enquiry." Same work. Completely different perceived value.

When you frame your skill in terms of the problem you solve — rather than the task you perform — something interesting happens to your pricing. People don't pay for tasks. They pay for outcomes. "I'll build you a chatbot" sounds like a task, and the client immediately starts comparing your price to other chatbot builders. "I'll help you capture the new patients you're currently losing" is an outcome, and the client starts calculating how much each lost patient is worth.

Same skill. Same work. Vastly different market rate.

Priya understood this intuitively. You can learn it deliberately. And once you see it, you can't unsee it.

* * *

Chapter 6: The Skills That Pay More Than They Should

Not all skills are created equal. I know that sounds obvious, but the implications are worth sitting with. Two people can work equally hard, for the same number of hours, with the same level of dedication, and one can earn five or ten times more than the other. The difference isn't effort. It's the skill itself – specifically, how closely that skill connects to making or saving someone money.

I want to walk through four skills that, right now, pay disproportionately well relative to how long they take to learn. These aren't the only ones. But they're the ones I've seen create the most opportunity for ordinary people starting from scratch.

Persuasive Writing

Every business needs words. Websites need copy. Emails need writing. Advertisements need headlines. Landing pages need text that convinces someone to click, buy, subscribe, or enquire. And here's the thing that makes this skill so valuable: most businesses are terrible at it.

They write about themselves. They use jargon their customers don't understand. They describe features when they should be describing outcomes. They have websites that look beautiful but say nothing compelling.

A person who can write words that make people take action – that's persuasive writing, or copywriting – is worth an absurd amount of money to the right business. Because the difference between a webpage that converts one in a hundred visitors and one that converts three in a hundred is often just the words. And that difference, in revenue terms, can be enormous.

You don't need an English degree to learn this. You need to understand a few core principles – how people make decisions, what makes them trust you, how to structure an argument that leads to action – and then practise them obsessively. Read what the best copywriters have written. Study ads that made you stop scrolling. Pay attention to the emails that made you click. The patterns are learnable.

The day-to-day of this skill looks like: talking to a business owner about their customers, understanding what those customers actually care about, and then writing words that bridge the gap between the two. It's research, empathy, and clear thinking, expressed in simple sentences. If you can write a clear email to a friend explaining why they should try a restaurant, you have the raw material for this skill.

System Implementation

Every industry runs on software. Dental practices use practice management software. Estate agents use CRM systems. Restaurants use booking platforms. Construction companies use project management tools. And almost universally, these businesses are using about twenty percent of what their software can do.

The opportunity here is not in building software. It's in becoming the person who sets it up, configures it, and makes it actually work for a specific type of business. This is what Priya did, though she might not have described it that way. She became the person who implemented specific tools for dental practices.

The key is specificity. Don't try to be an expert in all software for all businesses. Pick one tool and one industry. Become the person who knows that particular tool inside and out for that particular type of business. Learn every feature, every integration, every workaround. When someone in that industry has a problem with that system, you should be the person they think of.

This sounds narrow. It is. That's why it works. Narrow expertise commands premium prices because the client trusts that you understand their specific world. A generic "tech consultant" competes with millions of people. The person who specialises in setting up a particular CRM system for independent financial advisers competes with almost nobody.

Day-to-day, this looks like: learning a tool deeply through its documentation and practice, understanding the workflows of your chosen industry, setting up and configuring systems for clients, training their staff, and providing ongoing support. It's methodical, detail-oriented work. If you're the kind of person who enjoys getting systems to run smoothly, this could be your path.

AI Implementation

I almost hesitated to include this because the space is noisy. Everyone is talking about AI. But here's what I've observed: the gap between awareness and adoption is vast. Almost every business owner has heard of AI. Almost none of them are actually using it in any meaningful way. They know it exists. They suspect it could help them. They have no idea where to start.

That gap is the opportunity.

The person who can walk into a small business and say, "Let me show you three specific ways AI can save you ten hours a week," and then actually set those things up — that person is extraordinarily valuable right now. Not because AI is magic. But because the translation layer between what the technology can do and what businesses actually need is almost entirely missing.

This doesn't require a computer science degree. It requires understanding what current AI tools can do, staying reasonably up to date as they evolve, and having the ability to look at a business's daily operations and spot where automation would help. It's more about understanding people and processes than understanding algorithms.

The day-to-day: you'd be auditing how a business currently operates, identifying tasks that are repetitive or time-consuming, selecting the right AI tools for those tasks, setting them up, and teaching the team how to use them. Some of this involves chatbots and automated responses, like Priya's work. Some involves document processing, data analysis, content creation, or workflow automation. The specifics vary. The principle is constant: make the business run better with less manual effort.

Right now, this skill is in a golden window. The tools are good enough to deliver real value but new enough that most people haven't figured out how to use them. That window won't stay open forever. But it's wide open today.

Conversion-Focused Design

Here's something I learned the expensive way: a beautiful website and an effective website are not the same thing. I once paid a designer a significant amount to build me a gorgeous site. It looked stunning. People complimented it constantly. It generated almost no business. The design was a work of art. The conversion rate was a disaster.

Conversely, some of the highest-performing websites I've seen are frankly ugly by design standards. But they're structured in a way that guides visitors toward a specific action – a purchase, an enquiry, a sign-up. Every element has a purpose. Every section answers a question or addresses an objection. The layout isn't pretty for the sake of pretty. It's engineered to convert.

The person who can make something that looks good and converts well is rare. Most designers focus on aesthetics. Most marketers focus on conversion. The person who does both commands a premium that neither can match individually.

This skill involves understanding visual hierarchy – what people look at first, second, third on a page. It involves understanding buyer psychology – what makes someone trust you, what makes them hesitate, what pushes them over the edge to take action. And it involves the technical ability to build or modify pages that put all of this into practice.

Day-to-day, it means working with businesses to redesign their key pages — usually their homepage, their service pages, and their contact or checkout process. You'd analyse what's currently not working, propose changes based on conversion principles, implement them, and then measure the results. When you can show a business that your redesign increased their enquiries by a meaningful amount, you become very hard to replace.

Each of these four skills shares something in common. They can be learned in weeks or months, not years. They're directly connected to revenue — they help businesses make or save money. And they can be practised alongside a day job, with real clients, almost immediately.

I want to add one more thing about these skills, because I know what some of you are thinking. "But won't AI replace all of these?" It's a fair question. And my honest answer is: possibly, eventually, for some of them. But here's what I've observed. The skills that involve understanding people — their fears, their desires, their reluctance to change — are the last ones that technology will replace. A machine can write a decent email. It cannot yet sit across from a nervous business owner and understand what they're really worried about. It cannot read the room in a client meeting and adjust its approach. It cannot build trust.

The skills I've described above are not purely technical. They all require a deep understanding of human behaviour applied through a technical medium. That combination is remarkably durable.

You don't need to master all four. You don't even need to master one. You need to become competent enough in one of them to deliver value, and then improve through repetition. The mastery comes from doing, not studying.

* * *

Chapter 7: The Compound Effect of Skill Stacking

You don't need to be the best in the world at anything.

I want you to sit with that for a moment, because it contradicts almost everything you've been told about success. We're taught that excellence means being number one. The best writer. The best designer. The best salesperson. And if you can't be the best, what's the point?

But the world doesn't actually reward singular excellence as much as you'd think. The best copywriter in the world is making good money, sure. But you know who might be making more? Someone who is a reasonably good copywriter, a reasonably good data analyst, and has a solid understanding of one specific industry. Not the best at any of those things. But unusually good at the combination.

This is skill stacking. And it might be the most underappreciated concept in building wealth.

The idea is simple. Instead of trying to reach the top one percent of one skill — which takes years and often requires some natural talent — you aim for the top twenty-five percent of two or three skills that complement each other. That combination is rare. And rarity is what commands premium prices.

Here is how to visualise it:

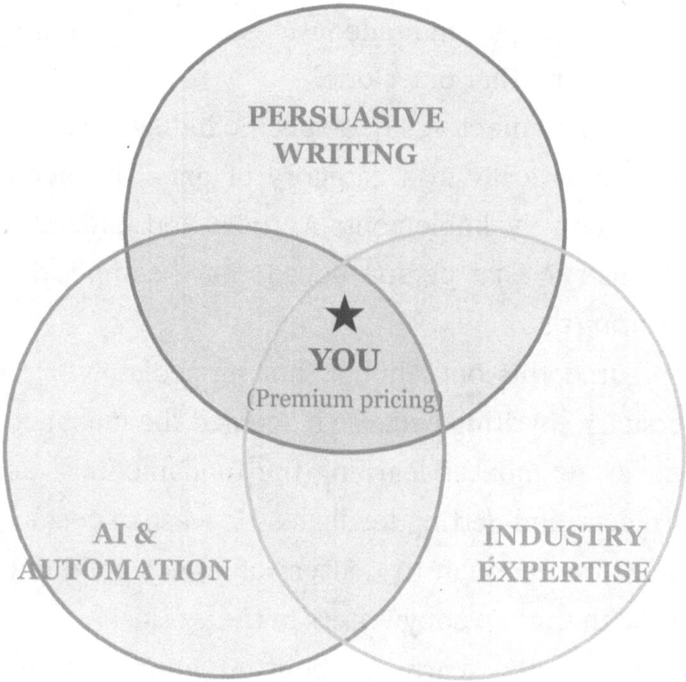

Each circle on its own is crowded. Thousands of people can write. Thousands understand AI tools. Thousands know a specific industry. But the overlap — the centre where all three meet — is nearly empty. That is where you want to stand.

Think about it mathematically. Being in the top twenty-five percent of one skill puts you ahead of most people in that area. That's good, but it's not particularly scarce. There are lots of competent writers, lots of capable designers, lots of decent salespeople.

But being in the top twenty-five percent of writing and the top twenty-five percent of AI implementation? Now you're in much rarer territory. The number of people who are good at both of those things simultaneously is a tiny fraction of those who are good at either one alone.

Add a third element – say, a specific industry knowledge – and you're practically in a category of one. The person who writes persuasively, implements AI tools, and understands the dental industry? That person doesn't have competition. They have a waiting list.

Alex figured this out, though not immediately. He started with persuasive writing because it seemed the most accessible. He spent a few months learning the fundamentals, taking on small projects, and getting feedback. He wasn't spectacular. He was solid. Good enough to deliver value, not good enough to compete with the top copywriters in the world.

Then he started learning about AI implementation. Not everything about AI. Just the practical side – which tools existed, what they could do, and how to set them up for small businesses. Again, he wasn't a world expert. He was competent and getting better.

Within eight months, Alex had a combination that was genuinely uncommon. He could help businesses write their marketing materials and automate parts of their operations using AI tools. Each skill on its own was fine. Together, they were worth significantly more than the sum of their parts.

His first major client was a recruitment firm that needed better job advertisements and a more efficient way to screen applications. Alex rewrote their ads to attract more qualified candidates and set up an AI-powered screening tool that saved the firm roughly fifteen hours a week. Neither task was revolutionary on its own. But the fact that one person could do both made Alex the obvious choice over hiring a separate copywriter and a separate tech consultant.

The fee he charged for that project was more than he'd have been comfortable asking for either skill individually. The client paid it without negotiating because the combined value was clear and substantial.

This is where the compound effect lives. Not in one extraordinary skill, but in the intersection of two or three complementary ones. That intersection is where scarcity lives. And scarcity is what creates premium pricing.

I should be clear about something: skill stacking isn't about collecting random abilities like stamps in a passport. The skills need to relate to each other. Writing and design complement each other naturally. AI implementation and industry expertise complement each other. Sales ability and technical knowledge complement each other. But writing and, say, juggling? That's not a stack. That's a hobby and a skill with no connection between them.

The question to ask yourself is: what two or three skills, combined, would make me unusually useful to a specific type of business? Not to everyone. To a specific type. The more specific, the more powerful the stack becomes.

You might not know the answer yet. That's fine. Start with one skill. Get competent. Then look around and ask: what would make this skill more valuable? What could I add to this that would make the combination rare? The second skill often reveals itself naturally once you're in the market, talking to clients, and seeing what they actually need.

Alex didn't plan his stack in advance. He stumbled into it by paying attention. He noticed that his writing clients kept asking about AI, and his AI work kept requiring good copy. The market showed him the intersection. He just had the sense to stand in it.

The compound effect of skill stacking works the same way as compound interest in investing. Each addition multiplies the value of what came before. Your first skill gives you a foundation. Your second skill multiplies it. Your third might multiply it again. And the longer you develop these complementary abilities, the wider the gap becomes between you and anyone who has only one of them.

Here's one more way to think about it. Imagine you're a small business owner and you need help. You could hire a writer to fix your website copy. Then you'd need to hire a separate consultant to help with AI tools. Then you'd need to find someone who understands your industry to make sure everything fits together. Three people, three relationships, three invoices, three sets of miscommunications.

Or you could hire one person who does all three – maybe not as brilliantly as each individual specialist, but well enough, and with the massive advantage of everything being joined up. One person who understands your business, writes your marketing, and sets up your systems. For most small businesses, that person is worth more than the three specialists combined, simply because of the coherence.

That's the quiet advantage of skill stacking. You're not competing on depth. You're competing on breadth and integration. And in a world full of narrow specialists, the person who can connect the dots across two or three disciplines is the one who becomes indispensable.

You don't need to be extraordinary. You need to be unusual. And "unusual" is much more achievable than you think.

* * *

Part III: The Digital Economy

Chapter 8: Building an Audience (Without Being Famous)

There is a piece of advice that floats around the internet like a persistent cold. It goes something like this: build an audience first, then figure out how to make money from it later.

I think this is backwards.

Not completely wrong. Just backwards. Because it encourages people to spend months or even years creating content with no commercial intent, and then wonder why nobody buys anything when they finally try to sell. The audience was built on entertainment, not trust around a specific problem. So when the pitch comes, it feels jarring. Like a friend who suddenly asks you to join a pyramid scheme.

Here is what I have seen work better. You build the audience and the offer at the same time. Not aggressively. Not with every post screaming "buy my thing." But with intention. You talk about a specific problem. You demonstrate you understand it deeply. And quietly, in the background, you build something that solves it. The audience grows around the problem, and when you present the solution, it feels natural. Like the obvious next step.

But let me back up. Because before we talk about strategy, I want to address the biggest shift that has happened in the last few years. And most people have not caught up to it.

The follower barrier has collapsed.

It used to be that social media platforms showed your content primarily to people who already followed you. If you had fifty followers, fifty people might see your post. If you had fifty thousand, fifty thousand might see it. This created a brutal chicken-and-egg problem. You needed followers to get reach, but you needed reach to get followers.

That world is gone. Platforms now run on interest-based algorithms. They show content to people based on what those people engage with, not who they follow. A brand new account with zero followers can publish something today and have it seen by tens of thousands of people tomorrow. I have watched this happen. Not once. Repeatedly.

This changes everything. It means your first piece of content has a genuine chance of reaching people. Not a guarantee, but a chance. And that chance compounds with volume.

Which brings me to the framework I use when thinking about content. I call it Hook-Arc-Shift, though I am sure someone smarter has a better name for it.

The Hook is the first few seconds. It is the thing that stops someone mid-scroll. It is not clickbait. It is curiosity. A question they had not considered. A statement that contradicts what they assumed. "Most people think saving money is about discipline. It is actually about environment." That is a hook. It creates a small gap in the mind that wants to be closed.

The Arc is the middle. The story, the argument, the explanation. This is where you demonstrate that you actually know what you are talking about. You share an example. You walk through the logic. You make the reader or viewer feel like they are learning something real, not being sold to.

The Shift is the ending. It is the insight that changes how they think about the topic. Not just information, but perspective. They walked in thinking one thing and walk out thinking something slightly different. That shift is what makes people remember you. It is what makes them come back.

Now here is the part that most people do not want to hear. Volume matters more than virality.

I have watched people agonise over a single piece of content for two weeks. Polishing every word. Adjusting the thumbnail. And then it gets forty views and they are crushed. Meanwhile, someone else publishes something rough and imperfect every single day, and by their fortieth piece, they are getting consistent traction.

Commit to one hundred pieces. Not one viral hit. Your hundredth piece will be dramatically better than your first. Not because you read more books about content creation, but because you developed an intuition for what resonates. You cannot get that intuition without reps.

I should also say this clearly: you do not need to show your face. This is a real barrier for many people, and it is entirely unnecessary. AI voiceover tools are now remarkably good. Screen recordings with a clear script work brilliantly in many niches. Some of the most successful educational channels I have seen are nothing more than well-written scripts over simple visuals. The camera is optional. The clarity of your thinking is not.

If I were starting from zero today, here is exactly what I would do. I would pick one platform. Just one. I would study what is already working in my topic area for about a week. Then I would post every single day for ninety days. Not ninety days of hoping. Ninety days of studying what works, adjusting, and improving.

At the end of those ninety days, I would evaluate honestly. What got traction? What fell flat? What felt sustainable? Then I would make decisions based on evidence, not assumptions.

The audience you need is smaller than you think. You do not need a million followers. You need a thousand people who trust you about a specific thing. That is enough to build a real income. And in a world where the algorithm will show your work to interested strangers for free, getting to a thousand is more achievable than it has ever been.

You just have to start. And you have to keep going past the silence of the first few weeks, when it feels like you are talking into an empty room.

You probably are. But the room fills faster than you expect.

* * *

Chapter 9: Leverage Products — Build Once, Sell Forever

I want to tell you about David. He is an accountant in Manchester. Not a famous one. Not a particularly remarkable one, by his own admission. He has been doing tax returns and bookkeeping for small businesses for about fifteen years.

One evening, after answering the same question from the third client that week — "How do I actually know if I can afford to hire someone?" — he had a thought. He had been answering the same twenty questions for fifteen years. Different clients, different businesses, but the same twenty questions.

So he set up his phone on a stack of books, opened a spreadsheet he had already built for himself, and recorded himself answering each question. No fancy editing. No intro music. Just David, his spreadsheet, and clear explanations. He bundled it into a simple course, listed it on a platform for forty-nine pounds, and shared it in a few Facebook groups for small business owners.

Seven people bought it the first month. He made three hundred and forty-three pounds. He almost forgot about it.

Six months later, without any additional promotion, it was selling fifteen to twenty copies a month. Word of mouth. Search engines. People finding it and telling other people. Within a year, the income from this course had overtaken what he earned from a meaningful chunk of his accounting clients.

David did not have an audience. He did not have tech skills. He had domain expertise about a specific problem that real people were willing to pay to solve.

This is what a leverage product is. It is something you build once and sell repeatedly, with essentially zero additional cost per sale. A guide. A template. A toolkit. A course. A set of resources. The economics are fundamentally different from services, because there is no scheduling involved. No trading hours. While you sleep, someone in another time zone can buy it, download it, and use it.

The most common mistake I see is people creating what they think people want, rather than what people demonstrably want. There is a difference. What you think people want is coloured by your own interests and assumptions. What people actually want is visible in their behaviour. What are they already searching for? What are they already buying? What questions do they keep asking in forums and groups?

The research process does not need to be complicated. Spend a week looking at what is already selling in your area of knowledge. Browse marketplaces. Read reviews – especially the negative ones, because those tell you what is missing. Look at the gaps. Not the topics that nobody is covering, but the topics that are being covered poorly.

Narrow focus wins almost every time. "Productivity course" is a losing proposition. There are thousands of them, made by people with bigger audiences and bigger budgets. But "Notion systems for solo consultants" – that is specific. That is a person with a specific problem looking for a specific solution. And when they find yours, the competition is minimal because most people are too busy trying to appeal to everyone.

The narrower you go, the less competition you face and the more you can charge. This seems counterintuitive. Surely a broader topic means more potential buyers? In theory, yes. In practice, a broad topic means you are invisible. A narrow topic means you are the obvious choice for a smaller but very motivated group.

Pricing is where most people sabotage themselves. They think about how long it took to create the product and try to charge accordingly. This is the wrong framework. A guide that took you a weekend to write might save someone twenty hours of confusion and help them avoid a costly mistake. The value is not in your creation time. It is in the problem solved.

If your product saves a small business owner ten hours a month, and their time is worth fifty pounds an hour, you are saving them five hundred pounds a month. Charging a hundred pounds for that is not expensive. It is an obvious decision. Price based on the value of the problem, not the hours you spent at your desk.

One more thing about leverage products. They compound in a way that services never can. David's course kept selling while he worked on other things. He eventually made a second course, then a third. Each one added a layer of income that required no additional time. After two years, he had four products generating a combined income that let him reduce his client load to three days a week.

He did not quit his accounting practice. He did not need to. He just had options. And options, as we discussed earlier, are the real definition of wealth.

The starting point is simpler than you think. What do you know that other people ask you about? What have you figured out through experience that someone earlier in the journey would pay to learn? Write it down. Record it. Package it. Put a price on it. Put it in front of the people who need it.

It will not make you rich next month. But it might change your financial trajectory entirely.

* * *

Chapter 10: Services and the Agency Ladder

If leverage products are the long game, services are the fast game. And sometimes, you need fast.

I have seen people go from zero income to their first paying client in less than two weeks. Not because they were brilliant. Not because they got lucky. Because services have the shortest distance between "I can do this" and "someone will pay me to do this."

Think about it. A leverage product needs to be built, polished, listed, and marketed before you see a single pound. An audience takes months of consistent effort. But a service? You find someone who has a problem, you solve it, and they pay you. The cycle can be extraordinarily short.

Here is the typical progression I have seen play out for people who take this path seriously.

In the first three months, you learn a marketable skill and build a handful of samples. These do not need to be paid work. They can be projects you do for yourself, for friends, for local businesses willing to let you help for free in exchange for a testimonial. Your first real client often comes through your personal network. Not because networking is magic, but because people prefer to hire someone they have some connection to, even a loose one.

Between months three and six, things start to take shape. You have three to five clients. You have raised your prices at least once, probably feeling uncomfortable about it. Your portfolio is filling up with real work and real results. You are starting to understand what the market actually values, which is almost never what you initially assumed.

From month six to twelve, you specialise. You pick a niche and go deep. Instead of offering "social media management" to anyone who will listen, you offer "Instagram content for independent restaurants" or "LinkedIn strategy for B2B consultants." The narrower you get, the more you can charge and the easier clients are to find. This is the same principle as leverage products. Specificity wins.

By the second year, you face a choice. You can stay solo, raise your prices further, and keep things lean. Or you can bring on help, start delegating, and build something that looks more like an agency. Both paths are valid. Neither is inherently better.

But I want to focus on something that happens in the middle of this journey, because it changes everything. The retainer shift.

Early on, most freelancers charge per project. Someone needs a website, you quote a price, you build it, they pay you, and then you need to find the next project. This creates a feast-or-famine cycle that is exhausting. Some months are flush, others are terrifyingly quiet.

The retainer model fixes this. Instead of one-off projects, you offer an ongoing monthly service. Content creation. Maintenance. Strategy. Management. Whatever makes sense for your skill. Five clients on a retainer of fifteen hundred pounds a month gives you seventy-five hundred pounds in predictable monthly income. That predictability changes your psychology. You stop operating from scarcity. You start making better decisions.

There is another model I want to describe, because I think it is underappreciated. I call it the middleman model, though that word carries unfair baggage. Here is how it works.

You find a client who needs a service. You find a specialist who can deliver that service. You manage the relationship, the communication, and the quality control. The client pays you. You pay the specialist. You keep the margin.

This sounds like it should not work. Why would the client not just hire the specialist directly? Because finding reliable specialists is hard. Managing them is hard. Ensuring quality is hard. The client is busy running their business. They want the problem solved, not another management headache. You provide genuine value by being the reliable, communicative middle layer.

And the specialist benefits too. They get to focus on what they are good at – the actual work – without having to chase clients, send invoices, or sit through briefing calls. You handle all of that.

I have watched people build substantial businesses on this model alone. No special skills of their own beyond project management and relationship building. They connect people and make sure things get done. The margins are real, the overhead is low, and the model scales.

But perhaps the most underrated benefit of the services path is the education it gives you. When you work directly with clients, you learn what people actually value. Not what business books say they value. Not what trends suggest they should value. What they will actually open their wallets for.

This education is priceless if you later want to build products or partnerships. You understand the market at a visceral level because you have been in the trenches with real customers. Every frustration, every request, every piece of feedback is data. And that data makes everything else you do smarter.

Services versus Products: Which Suits You?

This is not a question of which is better. It is a question of which fits your temperament.

	Services	Products
Speed to income	Fast — weeks	Slow — months
Income ceiling	Limited by your time	Unlimited (scales without you)
Client interaction	Constant	Minimal after launch
Predictability	Depends on client flow	Depends on market demand
Creative control	Shared with clients	Entirely yours
Personality fit	People who thrive on variety, relationships, and solving different problems	People who prefer building systems, working alone, and optimising

If you are energised by conversations, enjoy solving different problems every week, and feel restless without human interaction in your work — services will suit you. You will find the product path lonely and the long build phase frustrating.

If you are drained by client calls, prefer deep focus over switching between tasks, and get satisfaction from building something once that works repeatedly — products will suit you. You will find services exhausting and the constant client management draining.

Most people are not purely one or the other. But you lean one way. Be honest about which, and start there. You can always add the other later once the first is working.

Services are not glamorous. Nobody writes breathless articles about someone who manages Instagram accounts for dentists. But I know people doing exactly that who earn more than most junior doctors. They just do not talk about it much.

Which, if you think about it, is perfectly on brand for this book.

* * *

Part IV: The New Leverage

Chapter 11: AI as a Force Multiplier

I need to start this chapter with a correction. Because if you have been anywhere near the internet in the last couple of years, you have been told that AI is going to make you rich.

It is not.

AI is not a business model. It is not a money-printing machine. It is not going to replace the need for you to think clearly, work consistently, or build real relationships. If you take nothing else from this chapter, take that.

What AI actually is, when used well, is a force multiplier.

Let me explain what I mean with an analogy. When factories first got electric power in the early nineteen hundreds, it did not create businesses out of thin air. Nobody looked at an electric motor and said, "Brilliant, now I am rich." What it did was make existing businesses dramatically more efficient. Tasks that took ten people could now be done by three. Processes that took days could happen in hours. The businesses that understood this early pulled ahead. The ones that ignored it or misunderstood it fell behind.

AI is having a similar effect right now. It does not create value from nothing. It amplifies the value you already create.

I want to be specific about what AI actually does well, because the hype has made it hard to see clearly.

AI is remarkably good at research and synthesis. Need to understand a market, summarise a set of documents, or pull insights from a large amount of information? It can do in minutes what would take you hours. Not perfectly – you still need to check and think – but the speed difference is staggering.

It is good at producing first drafts. Not final drafts. First drafts. The difference matters. A first draft that is seventy percent of the way there saves you enormous time, because the editing and refining stage is faster than the blank-page stage. Most people I know who use AI well use it this way. It gets the clay on the table. They sculpt it into shape.

It is excellent at automating repetitive decisions. If you find yourself doing the same evaluation, the same sorting, the same categorisation over and over, AI can often handle this with minimal oversight.

And it is increasingly useful for pattern recognition. Finding trends in data, identifying what is working in your content, spotting anomalies in your business performance.

Here is what AI cannot do. It cannot build trust. People buy from people they trust, and trust is built through consistency, honesty, and genuine human connection over time. No algorithm replicates this.

It cannot exercise judgment in novel situations. When something genuinely new happens – a difficult client, an unexpected market shift, a moral dilemma – you need human judgment. AI can give you options. It cannot tell you which one aligns with your values.

And it cannot guarantee outcomes. Using AI does not mean your content will work, your product will sell, or your business will succeed. It just means you will be faster at the things that support those outcomes.

Let me tell you about Marcus. He dropped out of college at twenty and started a small content business. Nothing fancy. He researched topics, wrote scripts, recorded videos, and earned from a combination of ad revenue and affiliate recommendations.

Before AI tools became accessible, his bottleneck was research and writing. He could produce maybe three to four pieces of content a week. The research took half a day. The writing took another half day. Recording and editing took the rest.

When he started using AI for research and first drafts, his mornings became dramatically more productive. He would give the AI a topic, review and refine the research it produced, then work from the draft it generated. His afternoons stayed the same – recording, editing, publishing. But his output tripled. He went from three or four pieces a week to ten or twelve.

The revenue followed. Not immediately, but within a few months, his monthly income went from unpredictable – some months good, some months terrible – to reliably above ten thousand pounds. Same person. Same skills. Same audience. Just dramatically more efficient at the preparation stage.

The practical approach I recommend is simple. Map your workflow from start to finish. Every step, every task, every recurring activity. Then go through each one and ask: could AI handle eighty percent of this? Not a hundred percent. Eighty percent. Because that remaining twenty percent – the judgment, the editing, the human touch – is where your value lives.

I should be honest about one more thing. The window of advantage is narrowing. Right now, the people who understand and use these tools effectively have a meaningful edge. But the tools are getting easier and more accessible every month. What feels like a superpower today will feel like a baseline expectation in a couple of years.

This is not a reason to panic. It is a reason to start now, while the advantage is real and meaningful. The people who learn to work with AI early will have developed instincts and workflows that newcomers will struggle to replicate quickly.

Think of AI as your most eager but least experienced employee. It will work tirelessly, produce enormous volume, and never complain. But it needs supervision. It needs editing. And it needs you to set the direction.

The direction is still yours.

* * *

Chapter 12: The Invisible Partner Model

I stumbled onto this idea by accident, and I think it might be one of the most interesting opportunities available to ordinary people right now.

Here is the observation. There are millions of people on the internet who have built small but engaged audiences. Not millions of followers. Five thousand. Ten thousand. Maybe fifty thousand. They post regularly. Their followers comment, share, and genuinely care about what they have to say.

And most of them have nothing to sell.

Think about that. They have done the hardest part – building trust with a group of people – and they are leaving money on the table because they do not know how to commercialise it. Or they do not want to. They are creative people. They love making content, teaching, entertaining. The business side – building products, handling payments, writing sales pages, managing launches – feels foreign and uncomfortable.

This is where you come in.

The model is straightforward. You approach a creator and propose a partnership. You handle everything on the business side. Product creation, launch strategy, sales infrastructure, customer support. They continue doing what they already do well — creating content and engaging their audience. When sales come in, you split the revenue.

The maths are compelling. Let us say a creator has twenty thousand engaged followers. A well-matched product priced at two hundred pounds converts even modestly — say fifty buyers from a single launch. That is ten thousand pounds. If your split is thirty percent, you have earned three thousand pounds from one partnership, one launch.

Now imagine you have five such partnerships. Each launching a couple of times a year. The numbers add up quickly. And here is the important part: each new partnership adds income without proportionally increasing your workload. Because you are building systems. The sales page template gets refined. The launch sequence gets smoother. The customer support process gets documented. By your fifth partnership, you are operating with efficiency that your first launch could not have imagined.

The conversation with creators is easier than you might expect. You are not asking them for money. You are offering to help them make money. That is a fundamentally different dynamic. Most creators know they should be monetising their audience somehow. They have just never had someone competent offer to handle it for them.

Let me show you how Alex applied this model over about eighteen months. His first partnership was with a fitness creator who had around eight thousand followers on social media. They built a simple home workout programme together — Alex handled the product design, the platform, the sales page, the email sequences. The creator mentioned it in her content a few times and answered questions from her audience.

The first launch made about four thousand pounds. Alex's cut was twelve hundred. Not life-changing. But proof that the model worked.

His second partnership was better. He had learned from the first launch. The product was more focused. The sales page was sharper. The launch sequence was tighter. They made seven thousand pounds.

By his fifth partnership, Alex had refined his systems to the point where onboarding a new creator took about a week of setup, and launches ran almost on autopilot. He was earning enough from his portfolio of partnerships to leave his day job. And crucially, most of his time was spent on the interesting parts – finding creators, understanding their audiences, designing products that actually solved problems – rather than grinding through repetitive administrative work.

I want to be honest about the caveats, because this model is not without friction.

Not every partnership works. Some creators are unreliable. They agree to promote the product and then go quiet. Others have audiences that are engaged for entertainment but have no interest in buying anything. A fitness creator whose audience follows them for funny gym videos is very different from one whose audience follows them for genuine training advice. The first audience wants to be entertained. The second wants results. Only the second will buy.

Picking the right partners is probably the single most important skill in this model. You want creators who are consistent, who communicate well, and whose audiences engage in ways that suggest buying intent. Comments like "where can I get this?" or "do you have a programme for this?" are gold. They signal demand that already exists.

You also need to be genuinely good at the business side. If you botch the product, fumble the launch, or let down the creator's audience, you damage their trust with their community. That is not something to take lightly. Their reputation is on the line alongside your income.

But when it works – when you find a reliable creator with an engaged audience and pair them with a product that genuinely helps their followers – the model is powerful. You have built a business without building an audience. You have created income without creating content. You have leveraged someone else's strengths to complement your own.

This is partnership in the truest sense. Not exploitation. Not shortcuts. Two people with different skills combining them to create something neither could build alone.

* * *

Part V: The Long Game

Chapter 13: The Surplus Engine — Putting It All Together

Every financial strategy, no matter how sophisticated, eventually reduces to one simple equation.

Income minus expenses equals surplus.

That is it. That is the engine. Everything else is detail.

The surplus is what you have left after you have paid for your life. And what you do with it determines your financial trajectory more than almost any other decision. You can let it sit idle. You can spend it on things that do not matter. Or you can deploy it deliberately into three buckets: reinvestment, investment, and reserves.

Reinvestment goes back into your income streams. Better tools. Education. Hiring help. Anything that increases your capacity to earn. This is the bucket that grows your active income.

Investment goes into assets that grow on their own. We will talk about this in a moment.

Reserves are your safety net. Cash you can access quickly if something goes wrong. Three to six months of expenses is the usual guidance, and I think it is right. Not because disaster is likely, but because knowing you can survive a bad stretch changes how you make decisions. You stop accepting bad clients out of desperation. You stop staying in situations that drain you. The reserve buys you the ability to say no.

Let me talk about the income side first, because that is where most of the earlier chapters have been pointing. You now have several paths available. Services, leverage products, content, partnerships, some combination of these. The right mix depends entirely on your temperament and circumstances.

If you are someone who thrives on human interaction and quick feedback, services might be your primary path. If you are a builder who loves creating things and letting them work in the background, leverage products might suit you better. If you are a connector who sees opportunities between people, the partnership model might be your strength.

You do not need all of them. You need one that works, and then perhaps a second for diversification. Trying to do everything simultaneously is a recipe for doing nothing well.

Now, expenses. I am not going to tell you to stop buying coffee. That advice is insulting and mathematically irrelevant. The latte is not why you are not wealthy.

What I will say is this. There is a difference between intentional spending and unconscious spending. Intentional spending is when you genuinely choose to spend money on something that materially improves your life. A good meal with people you love. A tool that saves you hours. A holiday that restores your energy. I am all for this. Spend lavishly on what genuinely matters to you.

Unconscious spending is everything else. The subscriptions you forgot about. The upgrades you did not notice. The lifestyle inflation that crept in when your income rose. This is the spending worth examining. Not with guilt, but with curiosity.

Here is a practical exercise. Go through your bank statements for the last three months. Every recurring charge, every significant purchase. For each one, ask a single question: does this materially improve my life? Not "is this nice to have." Not "did I enjoy it briefly." Does it materially improve my life? The honest answers will surprise you. They surprised me.

The lifestyle inflation trap deserves special attention because it is subtle and powerful. When your income increases — from a raise, a new client, a successful launch — there is an almost gravitational pull towards spending more. A nicer flat. A better car. More dinners out. Each individual upgrade seems reasonable. But collectively, they consume the entire increase. Your income went up by a thousand pounds a month, and somehow your surplus stayed the same.

The antidote is a rule, and rules only work if they are simple. Here is mine: every time my income increases, at least half of the increase goes to the gap between income and expenses. Not all of it. I am not a monk. But at least half. This means my surplus grows every time my income grows, even as my lifestyle improves somewhat.

Now let us talk about investing, and I am going to keep this deliberately simple because I think the investment industry has made things unnecessarily complicated in order to justify its fees.

If you are not an expert — and statistically, you are not, and neither am I — broad index funds are your friend. An index fund owns a tiny slice of hundreds or thousands of companies at once. You do not need to pick winners. You do not need to follow markets. You do not need to have opinions about interest rates or economic cycles.

You set up a monthly automatic transfer. The money goes in. You forget about it. You do this for decades.

The maths of patience are striking. Most of the growth in a long-term investment happens in the final years, because compounding is exponential, not linear. The first decade feels slow. The second feels better. The third feels extraordinary. The person who started ten years earlier than you is not just ten years ahead — they might be several multiples ahead, because of how compounding works in later years.

This is why starting matters more than amount. Someone who invests a modest sum monthly for thirty years will almost certainly end up with more than someone who invests a large sum monthly for ten years. Time is the multiplier.

Here is where the earlier chapters connect. If you are building income from services, products, or partnerships, your surplus is not limited to the margin from a single salary. It can grow. And as it grows, you can make larger monthly investments into the same vehicle. Same index fund. Same automatic transfer. Just a bigger number. The destination does not change. The journey gets shorter.

I want to address multiple income streams directly, because there is a lot of noise about this topic. Having multiple streams of income is genuinely valuable. Not because each one makes you rich, but because diversity provides safety. If one stream falters – a client leaves, a product stops selling, a partnership ends – the others keep you afloat while you rebuild.

But there is an important nuance. Do not diversify prematurely. Get one stream working properly before adding a second. Get two working before adding a third. Each stream requires attention and energy, especially in the beginning. Spreading yourself too thin too early means nothing gets the focus it needs to succeed.

The final piece of the puzzle is systems. I have watched people build impressive income and then hit a ceiling because everything depends on them personally. They are the bottleneck. If they stop working, everything stops.

The way past this ceiling is documentation and delegation. Every process you do repeatedly should be written down clearly enough that someone else could execute it. Not perfectly – but well enough. Then you find someone to execute it, and you move your attention to the things that only you can do.

This is not about building a big company. It is about building a life where your income is not entirely dependent on your daily labour. Where the systems run, the investments compound, and your time increasingly belongs to you.

The Investing Conversation Nobody Has Honestly

I want to say something about investing that most books in this space avoid, because it does not sound inspiring. The truth is that investing is boring. Properly boring. If your investment approach is exciting, you are probably doing it wrong.

The financial industry makes its money by convincing you that investing is complicated. That you need active management, stock picking, market timing, sector rotation, and a hundred other strategies that sound sophisticated and charge high fees. The evidence, overwhelmingly, suggests that most of these approaches underperform a simple index fund over any meaningful time period.

This does not mean investing requires no thought at all. You should understand the basics: what an index fund is, how compound interest works, why diversification matters, and what your actual risk tolerance is (not what you think it is in a calm moment, but what it really is when markets drop and your balance shrinks). These are worth learning. They take perhaps a weekend of reading, not a finance degree.

But beyond those basics, the optimal strategy for most people is: automate, forget, and continue for decades. The person who checks their portfolio daily and adjusts based on news headlines will almost certainly underperform the person who set up an automatic monthly transfer five years ago and never logged in since.

I also want to be honest about what investing cannot do for you at the beginning. If you are investing a hundred pounds a month, compounding is working, but the numbers are small. After a year, you have roughly twelve hundred pounds plus a little growth. That is meaningful as a habit and a foundation. It is not going to change your life next month.

This is why the income-building chapters came first in this book. The fastest way to accelerate your investment timeline is not to find a better return. It is to increase the amount you invest. Going from a hundred a month to a thousand a month – which is entirely achievable once you have a functioning side income – changes everything about the trajectory.

Invest from day one. But do not expect investing alone to do the heavy lifting in the early years. Let your active income carry that weight while your investments quietly compound in the background.

The Emotional Side of Money

I have avoided talking about emotions for most of this book, because I think the advice space overindexes on mindset and underindexes on mechanics. But there is one emotional truth worth naming.

Building wealth is lonely in a specific way. Your friends will not always understand what you are doing. Some will think you are being irresponsible. Others will think you are being greedy. Most will simply not relate, because they have not made the same choice, and your progress makes them uncomfortable about their own inaction.

This is not a reason to stop. But it is worth knowing in advance, so it does not surprise you. Find one or two people who understand what you are building. Not a hundred. One or two. People who are on a similar path, who celebrate your wins genuinely, and who understand the specific frustration of building something in the margins.

This might be a friend. It might be someone in an online community. It might be a sibling or a partner. But having even one person who gets it makes the difference between sustainable effort and eventual burnout.

You do not need a crowd cheering for you. You need one person who nods.

That is the surplus engine. Income in. Intentional expenses out. Surplus deployed into reinvestment, investment, and reserves. Repeated consistently, adjusted as circumstances change, protected by diversification.

It is not exciting. It is not fast. It will not make for a compelling social media post.

But it works. Quietly, reliably, over time. Which, by now, should sound familiar.

* * *

CLOSING: YOUR FIRST HUNDRED DAYS

I have given you a lot in this book. Frameworks, stories, strategies, warnings. But I know from experience that information without action is just entertainment. You read it, you feel inspired for a day, and then normal life reasserts itself and nothing changes.

So let me give you something concrete. A hundred-day plan. Not because a hundred days is magic, but because it is long enough to see real results and short enough to feel manageable. It is also, roughly, the point at which a new habit becomes durable. After a hundred days, you are no longer forcing yourself. You are just doing the thing.

Days one through seven. Choose one path. Just one. Not two, not three. One. Maybe it is freelance services based on a skill you already have. Maybe it is building a leverage product around your expertise. Maybe it is growing an audience around a topic you know well. Maybe it is the partnership model, helping creators monetise.

Write it down. Physically write it on a piece of paper and put it where you will see it every morning. This is your commitment for the next hundred days. You are not allowed to switch. The grass will look greener on other paths – it always does – and you will resist the temptation because you made a decision and you are the kind of person who honours their decisions.

Days eight through twenty-one. Learn the fundamentals of your chosen path. Notice I said two weeks, not two months. This is not a university degree. You need to know enough to take the first real step, not enough to write a textbook.

If you chose services, spend these two weeks understanding your target market and building two or three sample projects. If you chose a product, spend them researching what people actually want and outlining what you will build. If you chose content, spend them studying what works on your chosen platform and scripting your first batch. If you chose partnerships, spend them identifying ten creators who might be a good fit.

Two weeks. Then you move.

Days twenty-two through thirty-five. Build your first asset. Not your final, perfect, polished asset. Your first one. A portfolio page. A sample product. A library of ten content pieces. A pitch document for potential partners.

This will be imperfect. It is supposed to be. Imperfect and existing beats perfect and imaginary every single time. You can improve it later. Right now, you need something tangible in the world.

Days thirty-six through seventy. This is the part where you put yourself in front of your market. You reach out to potential clients. You publish your content. You list your product. You contact creators.

This is also where most people quit.

The silence is normal. The first few weeks of outreach and publishing feel like shouting into a void. Nobody responds. Nobody buys. Nobody seems to notice. And the voice in your head says, "See? This does not work. You are not cut out for this. Go back to what you were doing before."

That voice is wrong. It is not lying — the silence is real. But it is drawing the wrong conclusion. The silence does not mean it will not work. It means it has not worked yet. Every person I know who has built something meaningful went through this phase. Every single one.

Push through it. Keep going. Keep improving. Keep showing up.

Days seventy-one through one hundred. Now you have data. Real data, not assumptions. Some things worked. Some did not. Some content got traction. Some fell flat. Some outreach got responses. Some was ignored.

This is where you iterate. Double down on what worked. Abandon what did not. Adjust your approach based on evidence. This is not failure. This is the scientific method applied to building a livelihood. Hypothesis, experiment, observation, adjustment.

By day one hundred, you will not be wealthy. Let me be clear about that. But you will have something that almost nobody has: momentum. A real project with real feedback. Skills that did not exist a hundred days ago. And proof – to yourself, which is the only audience that matters – that you can build something from nothing.

There is one more practice I want to suggest for these hundred days. I call it the Daily Compound. Every single day, take one meaningful action towards your goal. Not a busy action. Not reorganising your files or redesigning your logo for the third time. A meaningful action. Something that moves you closer to income, to clients, to audience, to partnerships.

One per day. Every day. For a hundred consecutive days.

It sounds small. It is not. A hundred meaningful actions compound in ways that are impossible to predict from the starting line. Each one builds on the last. Each one opens doors you could not have seen before. The version of you at day one hundred will look back at the version of you at day one and barely recognise them.

I started this book by saying that wealth is quieter than you have been told. That the people who build lasting financial freedom rarely look the part. They are not flashy. They are not loud. They do not have secrets or shortcuts or lucky breaks that explain everything.

What they have is simpler than that. They have a willingness to start before they feel ready. They have the stubbornness to continue when results are slow. They have the clarity to focus on what works and discard what does not. And they have the patience to let time do what time does – compound small actions into remarkable outcomes.

You do not need to be extraordinary to build an extraordinary life. You need to be consistent. You need to be intentional. And you need to be willing to play a longer game than most people around you.

Wealth is not reserved for the lucky. It is built by ordinary people who do one extraordinary thing: they start, and they do not stop.

This is your day one. Make it count.

* * *

What Happens After Day One Hundred

I want to tell you what comes next, because the hundred-day plan is a beginning, not an end. And the shape of the journey after those first hundred days is worth understanding, even if the specifics will differ for everyone.

Months four through six. You have momentum now. You know what works and what does not. The task is to deepen, not to diversify. Take whatever produced results in those first hundred days and double down on it. If outreach to a certain type of client worked, do more of it. If a certain style of content got traction, make more of it. This is not the time to get bored and chase something new. This is the time to exploit what you have learned.

Your income during this period will likely still be inconsistent. Some weeks will feel like a breakthrough. Others will feel like regression. This is normal. The trend matters more than any individual week. If the trend is upward – even slowly – you are on the right path.

Months six through twelve. This is when things start to feel real. The awkwardness of the early days fades. You stop feeling like an impostor and start feeling like a professional. Not because anything dramatic happened, but because repetition builds identity. You have been doing this thing for six months now. It is no longer a side project. It is part of who you are.

Financially, this is when the first meaningful milestones tend to arrive. Your first thousand-pound month. Then your first month where the side income covers a significant bill. Then a month where you realise you could, in theory, survive on this alone. You probably should not act on that realisation yet – the bridge needs to be stronger – but the knowledge changes your relationship with your day job. You are there by choice, not necessity. That psychological shift is worth more than the money.

Year two. You have options now. Real ones. Maybe you reduce your hours at work. Maybe you negotiate a different arrangement. Maybe you keep the job and use the extra income to invest aggressively, compressing the traditional wealth path from forty years to fifteen. Maybe you are ready to make the full jump.

The choice is yours. And having a choice is the whole point.

I have watched people at this stage make every possible decision. Some leave employment and never look back. Some keep their jobs because they genuinely enjoy the work and use the extra income for freedom in other areas – longer holidays, a nicer home, early retirement savings. Some scale aggressively and build teams. Some stay deliberately small.

None of these choices are wrong. The only wrong choice is the one you make from obligation rather than genuine preference. If you have built the gap – if your expenses are covered by income that does not require your constant presence – you have earned the right to choose based on what you actually want, not what circumstance demands.

The quiet life.

George, the man with the washing machines, never appeared on anyone's podcast. He never wrote a book. He never had a social media following. He lived in a modest house, drove his old car, and spent his time exactly as he pleased.

I think about him often. Not because his specific approach was revolutionary – washing machines in student halls is not exactly a Silicon Valley pitch deck – but because he understood something that most people never grasp. Wealth is not a performance. It is not something you display. It is something you live.

The wealth rewire is not just a strategy for building wealth. It is a philosophy for living with it. You build quietly. You grow quietly. And when you have enough – when the gap is wide and the pressure is gone and your time belongs to you – you live quietly too.

Unless you do not want to. Then you do whatever you like. Because you can.

That is freedom. And it is built one unglamorous day at a time.

* * *

The Wealth Rewire: Reprogram Your Brain for Passive Income

* * *

www.ingramcontent.com/pod-product-compliance
Lightning Source LLC
LaVergne TN
LVHW090330210926
848480LV00004B/1367
* 9 7 9 8 9 0 4 7 9 0 4 3 1 *